Zoo Animals

TOUCANS AT THE ZOO

By Seth Lynch

Please visit our website, www.garethstevens.com. For a free color catalog of all our high-quality books, call toll free 1-800-542-2595 or fax 1-877-542-2596.

Library of Congress Cataloging-in-Publication Data

Names: Lynch, Seth, author.
Title: Toucans at the zoo / Seth Lynch.
Description: New York : Gareth Stevens Publishing, [2020] | Series: Zoo animals | Includes index.
Identifiers: LCCN 2018039581| ISBN 9781538239544 (paperback) | ISBN 9781538239568 (library bound) | ISBN 9781538239551 (6 pack)
Subjects: LCSH: Toucans–Juvenile literature. | Zoo animals–Juvenile literature.
Classification: LCC QL696.P57 L96 2020 | DDC 598.7/2–dc23
LC record available at https://lccn.loc.gov/2018039581

First Edition

Published in 2020 by
Gareth Stevens Publishing
111 East 14th Street, Suite 349
New York, NY 10003

Editor: Therese Shea
Designer: Katelyn E. Reynolds

Photo credits: Cover, p. 1 buteo/Shutterstock.com; p. 5 rainyclub/Shutterstock.com; p. 7 (top left) DDCoral/Shutterstock.com; p. 7 (top right) Mike Price/Shutterstock.com; p. 7 (bottom left) Eric Isselee/Shutterstock.com; p. 7 (bottom right) apple2499/Shutterstock.com; p. 9 Surkov Vladimir/Shutterstock.com; p. 11 DeLoyd Huenink/Shutterstock.com; p. 13 Rodrigo Friscione/Image Source/Getty Images; pp. 15, 24 (bill) jo Crebbin/Shutterstock.com; pp. 17, 24 (tongue) Brian Lasenby/Shutterstock.com; p. 19 julianufer/Shutterstock.com; p. 21 Tacio Philip Sansonovski/Shutterstock.com; p. 23 Art Montes De Oca/Photographer's Choice/Getty Images.

Printed in the United States of America

CPSIA compliance information: Batch #CS19GS: For further information contact Gareth Stevens, New York, New York at 1-800-542-2595.

Contents

I see toucans at the zoo.
I learn a lot!

There are about
35 kinds of toucans.

The biggest is
the toco toucan.

Toucans live
in rain forests.

They live in tree holes.

They have a big bill.

They have
a long tongue.

They eat fruits.
They eat small animals.

They are loud!

I like toucans
at the zoo!

Words to Know

bill

tongue

Index